AUG   1985   JUNIOR

DATE DUE			
NOV 0 9 '95	MAY 30 '06		
JAN 0 2 '96	DEC 12 '07		
MAR 1 1 '96	JAN 27 '01		
DEC 0 6 1996			
FEB 1 1 '97	APR 1 4 '01		
APR 23 '97	MAY 23 '06		
JAN 1 3 '98			
MAR 06 '99			
MAR 0 1 '00			
MAY 0 2 '00			

Jackson

County

Library

System

HEADQUARTERS:

413 W. Main

Medford, Oregon   97501

GAYLORD M2G

SANDRA
DAY
O'CONNOR

SANDRA
DAY
O'CONNOR

BY CHRISTOPHER HENRY

A FIRST BOOK

FRANKLIN WATTS
New York / Chicago / London / Toronto / Sydney

Cover photographs copyright ©: Archive Photos: of The Collection
of the Supreme Court of the United States (inset)

Photographs copyright ©: Gamma-Liaison, Inc.: pp. 2 (Diana Walker), 6 (Theo
Westenberger), 45 (David Kennerly); North Wind Picture Archives, Alfred, Me.: p. 12;
The Smithsonian Institution: p. 15 (#2508); El Paso Public Library: p. 17 (Otis Aultman);
UPI/Bettmann: pp. 18, 20, 23, 28, 32, 36, 40, 47, 49; The Radford School, El Paso,
Tx.: p. 22; Austin High School Library: p. 25; Stanford University News Service: p. 26;
AP/Wide World Photos: pp. 30, 42; The Bettmann Archive: p. 34; Arizona Historical
Foundation: p. 39; The Collection of the Supreme Court of the United States: pp. 51, 56
(National Geographic); Reuters/Bettmann: p. 54.

Henry, Christopher.
Sandra Day O'Connor / Christopher Henry.
p. cm.
Includes bibliographical references and index.
ISBN 0-531-20175-9 (lib. bdg.)
1. O'Connor, Sandra Day 1930—Juvenile literature. 2. Women judges—United
States—Biography—Juvenile literature. 3. United States. Supreme Court—
Biography—Juvenile literature. [1. O'Connor, Sandra Day, 1930– . 2. Judges. 3.
Women—Biography. 4. United States. Supreme Court—Biography.] I. Title.
KF8745.O25H46 1994
347.73'2634—dc20
[B]
[347.3073534]
[B]   94-11287
CIP AC

For Jesse, my inspiration and best friend.

With love.

. . . I will bring the understanding of a woman to the Court, but I doubt that alone will affect my decisions. I think the important thing about my appointment is not that I will decide cases as a woman, but that I am a woman who will get to decide cases.

Judge Sandra Day O'Connor's response
to reporters' questions about her being
appointed the first woman to serve on the
U.S. Supreme Court

CONTENTS

SANDRA
DAY
O'CONNOR

BOUND FOR TEX

Sandra Day O'Connor's grandparents were among the thousands of Easterners who traveled west at the end of the 1800s in search of cheap land.

CHAPTER 1

APACHE COUNTRY

A s the first woman to be appointed to the U.S. Supreme Court, Sandra Day O'Connor will always occupy a special place in American history. From an independent family of pioneers who crossed the country to set up businesses on their own land, Sandra grew up on her family's cattle ranch on the Arizona–New Mexico border. As a child, she quickly learned the importance of self-reliance and developed an affection for the Arizona desert and countryside.

Sandra's grandfather, Henry Clay Day, had come to the Southwest from Vermont in the 1870s, about a decade after the Civil War had ended. At the age of twenty-one, he went to Wichita, Kansas, where he earned a sizable sum in the lumber business. While in the Midwest, Henry met and married a local woman, Alice Edith Hilton.

After their wedding, Henry and Alice Day headed further west to make their fortune in a new business venture — a ranch. Land was "dirt cheap" in southwest America then and they purchased a vast piece of it, some three hundred square miles in southeastern Arizona, equal in size to one-quarter the entire state of Rhode Island. The Days built an adobe house made of sun-dried clay bricks and named their ranch the "Lazy B," after the sloping "B" branded on their large herd of cattle by the previous owner.

Henry and Alice found life was not easy on the Lazy B ranch. The land was dry, barren, and useful only for grazing cattle. With no electricity or plumbing, they had to haul water from an outdoor pump. Alice had to act as the family doctor for most of her five children's illnesses. Miles away from their nearest neighbors, the family lived in almost complete isolation. But Henry was hardworking and enterprising, even building a small, separate building as a schoolroom for his children, and the family learned to rely on themselves.

At that time, the threat of attack by hostile Indians was ever-present. The Indians were angry at the white settlers, who now claimed land the Indians believed was rightfully theirs — land they had lived on for hundreds of years before the white people had ever come to North America. Geronimo, the unmerciful Apache chief, led his raiding parties against many local ranches, killing some white settlers. Henry and Alice Day were both handy with firearms, and they taught their children at an early age how to use a gun safely. The Days were well armed in case Geronimo decided to come calling, which he did on a few occasions. Fortunately, the family lost only a few horses instead of their lives.

Geronimo directed many raids against white settlers in the southwestern United States during the 1870s and 1880s. This well-known photograph of the Apache warrior was taken in 1886.

Sandra Day O'Connor's father, Harry Day, was born at the Lazy B in 1899. By then, even the stubbornly independent Henry Day had realized that his one-room schoolhouse could not provide his children with a real education, so he and Alice took their family to Pasadena, California. Young Harry attended school there and hoped to enroll at Stanford University, but his father died before Harry graduated from high school.

By this time, the Lazy B, which had been left in the hands of a foreman, was in severe financial trouble, and the Days were in danger of losing the property. The foreman, largely unsupervised, had run the business into the ground and owed a lot of money. Scrapping his plans for college, Harry Day returned home to the Lazy B to set the business right again. Ultimately, it took him most of a decade to fatten and sell enough cattle to pay off the Lazy B's debts.

Harry Day settled into a routine as a bachelor rancher for the next ten years. Putting in long hours at the Lazy B, he didn't have many opportunities to meet women. On a trip to buy some stock cattle from a man named Willis Wilkey, who lived in El Paso, Texas, Harry met the cattle trader's daughter, Ada Mae, and began a correspondence with her. Harry and Ada Mae were soon writing to each other almost daily. They had met only a half-dozen times, but knew they were right for each other. In 1927, on one of his weekend trips to El Paso, Harry asked Ada Mae to marry him. They ran off to New Mexico and were married

*Ada Mae Wilkey lived with her family in El Paso,
Texas (downtown shown here), before she met her
future husband, Harry Day. She returned there to give
birth to their first child, Sandra, in 1930.*

By the age of ten, Sandra already was an
accomplished horseback rider. This photo, taken
at the Lazy B, is from her scrapbook.

the following day. Then the young couple headed back to the Lazy B ranch and Harry's loneliness ended for good.

Three years later, Ada Mae became pregnant with their first child. She returned to El Paso to be close to a good hospital and her family, and on March 26, 1930, Sandra Day was born. The Days' next baby would not arrive until eight years later, so Sandra got a lot of adult attention as a little girl. Without any other children at the ranch, Sandra was sometimes lonely and had to use her imagination to entertain herself.

Of course, Sandra had a lot of advantages in her life. She had lots of land to explore and was given many adult responsibilities at a young age. She started reading at the age of four and some years later learned how to load, aim, and fire a rifle. In those days, guns were still a part of every-day life. Her father taught her how to ride a horse and drive a tractor before she was ten. She knew how to use tools, pick apples from the family's orchard at the peak of ripeness, and burn the Lazy B's mark onto her father's cattle with a branding iron. She also knew how to use make-up, wear a fancy dress, and walk gracefully in high heels, but Sandra was inclined to only on special occasions.

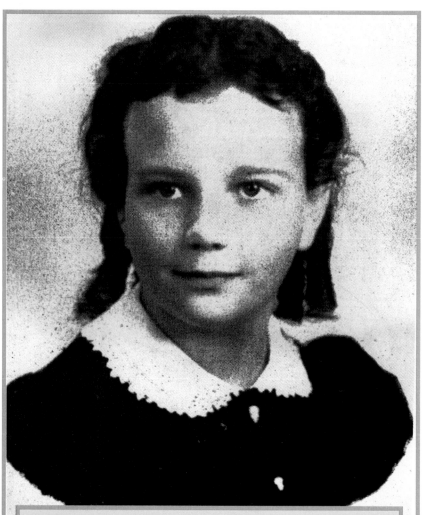

From the age of six, Sandra lived with her grandparents and went to the Radford School for Girls in El Paso, Texas. This is her third grade portrait.

CHAPTER 2

A FURTHER EDUCATION

Sandra loved the Lazy B ranch, despite all of its hardships, and hoped she would never have to leave. Sandra's mother, however, understood the limits of schooling her daughter at home. As a college graduate, unusual for women at that time, Ada Mae realized the importance of education and was determined that her daughter would have the best the Days could afford.

When Sandra was six years old, her parents sent her to live with Ada Mae's parents, Willis and Mamie Scott Wilkey, in El Paso. There, Sandra attended the Radford School for Girls, a private academy that taught both classical academic studies and the social skills necessary to move in privileged circles. Sandra, who could shoot a coyote between the eyes at forty paces, must have had mixed feelings about wearing a floor-length gown for an afternoon of ballroom dancing followed by a tea party. And at her young age, she also must have been very sad to leave her family and home.

Although Sandra stayed with her grandparents while

Sandra, third from left in the third row, appears with her classmates at the Radford School. The young boy second from left in the first row became a well-known television journalist in Washington, D.C. His name is Sam Donaldson.

Ada Mae Day and her children (from left to right:
Alan, Ann, and Sandra) pose for an Easter picture
at the Lazy B ranch in 1940.

school was in session, she spent most holidays, summer vacations, and long weekends with her family at the Lazy B ranch. When Sandra was eight, her first sibling, Ann, was born. Sandra was thrilled to have a sister. A year later, a brother, Alan, came along, and to Sandra it seemed as if the Days were finally an ordinary family. Ann and Alan were too young to be real playmates for Sandra, but she often looked after them for her mother.

After graduating from the Radford School for Girls a year early, Sandra Day enrolled at Austin High School in El Paso. At a public school, Sandra was no longer surrounded only by the daughters of the well-to-do, and her classmates were from every sort of background. Although she continued to live some two hundred miles away from her parents, Sandra behaved maturely and responsibly in high school, successfully juggling school activities and class work.

Sandra Day was one of Austin's top students, and her vigorous study habits paid off when she graduated. Only sixteen years old, she had applied for admission to only one school — Stanford University, then the "Harvard" of the western states. Stanford was tough to get into, especially for girls. But, Sandra knew what she wanted, and apparently so did the admissions people at the university who accepted her!

Sandra Day headed to college in September 1946. If she had found El Paso overwhelming, she must have

When Sandra graduated from high school in 1946, she was only sixteen years old. She went straight on to college and majored in economics, an unusual course of study for women at that time.

At Stanford, Sandra pursued a degree in law.
In 1950, she was elected senior-class president.

thought Stanford University, near San Francisco, truly intimidating. Some of the best students in the country were her classmates now, and Sandra must have wondered if she could compete with them. She need not have been concerned. Her independence helped her to thrive away from parental supervision and support, and her self-discipline assured her academic success.

After an introductory law course, Sandra transferred into a special program at Stanford that granted both undergraduate and law degrees in a combined six-year program. The opportunity to be a practicing attorney at the age of just twenty-two appealed to Sandra. Unfortunately, she had no idea how tough it would be for a young woman, even a well-qualified one, to find work as a lawyer.

When she graduated from Stanford Law School in the spring of 1952, Sandra was ranked third in her class in academic standing. The first-place student, a shy, down-to-earth World War II veteran named William Hubbs Rehnquist, would go on to join the U.S. Supreme Court in 1972 and become its Chief Justice in 1986. Sandra and Bill Rehnquist were friendly with each other in law school but had no idea of what their futures would hold. They certainly would have been shocked to know that they would one day serve together on the nation's highest court.

Normally, a Stanford Law School graduate who finished third would have been flooded with offers of well-

Sandra Day (second from left in the first row) was one of the few women in the class of 1952 at Stanford Law. Her graduating class included William H. Rehnquist (furthest left in the fourth row), now chief justice of the Supreme Court.

paying employment all over the country. Bill Rehnquist, for example, was hired as a clerk for Supreme Court Justice Robert Jackson, a position that laid the foundation for the rest of Rehnquist's career. Sandra Day, however, did not find any law firm that wanted to hire her as a lawyer. One of California's best law firms, after interviewing her and examining her superior credentials, did offer her a job — as a legal secretary!

Finally, in San Mateo, California, Sandra Day found a job as a law clerk with the county government. The position was not prestigious and the pay was poor, but Sandra didn't care; she had been accepted as a member of the legal profession.

This photo was taken in 1950, about the time Sandra met John O'Connor.

CHAPTER 3

MARRIAGE AND FAMILY LIFE

I n December 1952, Sandra Day married John Jay O'Connor III, a fellow Stanford law student one year behind her and a native of San Francisco. The two had met as editors working for the Stanford Law Review, a school journal that published articles about legal issues, and they immediately found much in common with each other. Their wedding was held at the Lazy B amid many family members and friends.

As he started his last semester of studies, John was drafted into the U.S. Army. At the time, the Korean War was drawing to a close, and American military forces were being built up in Europe. Upon graduation, John was assigned to the Judge Advocate General's Corps, the army's legal division, and sent to Germany. Sandra quit her job with San Mateo County and accompanied her husband overseas.

Sandra Day O'Connor settled into life as an army wife. She also found work as a civilian lawyer in the Quarter-

After World War II, many U.S. military personnel and their families, including the O'Connors, were stationed through-out West Germany. This picture shows American soldiers marching through the streets of West Berlin—located in East Germany but in fact part of West Germany.

master Corps, the division that handled army purchasing. The young couple made the most of their time in Europe and even found time for some ski trips.

Two years later, when John finished his tour of duty, the O'Connors returned to the United States and settled in Phoenix, Arizona. They bought a piece of land for a few thousand dollars and built a house. Both Sandra Day and John O'Connor were admitted to the bar in the state of Arizona, but only John was able to find a job with a good firm. By this time, Sandra was pregnant and mostly stayed home, waiting for the birth of her first son, Scott Hampton, who was born on October 8, 1957.

With the knowledge that most law firms would simply not hire a young mother, Sandra Day O'Connor decided to open a small law firm with a friend, Tom Tobin. The two young lawyers did anything and everything for a legal fee. Working on divorces, wills, estates, house closings, personal injuries, contracts, and even criminal cases helped them pay their bills and occasionally make a profit. However, running a law firm and building a client base is tough for any new lawyer, especially one who has to care for an infant child. In a few years, the law partners parted for good.

With the birth of the O'Connors' second son, Brian, in 1960, Sandra quit work for a few years. Two years later another child, son number three, Jay, was born. Now, with three boys under the age of five, Sandra wondered if she might have to give up the practice of law entirely and devote herself to raising her young family, which she did not find objectionable. Marriage and family life were just as important to Sandra Day O'Connor as her legal career could ever be.

Sandra Day O'Connor began her political career in the
Arizona State Senate in Phoenix, where she developed
a reputation for hard work and effectiveness.

CHAPTER 4

POLITICS
AND THE LAW

Although she was busy at home as a full-time mother from 1960 to 1965, Sandra Day O'Connor became active in local politics. She volunteered as a county committee member for the Republican party for four years and served on several important government commissions. In 1965, Sandra found a part-time position as an assistant attorney general for the state and worked as a prosecutor. She was tough and relentless in her duties but respected by criminal defense attorneys.

In 1969, Sandra Day O'Connor left the office of the *state attorney general* for a career in politics. A Republican-held seat in the Arizona State Senate had become vacant, and the party's leaders appointed O'Connor to finish the rest of the term of office. Only seventeen years after having been first turned away by the legal profession, Sandra Day O'Connor now held a seat in the Arizona *state legislature*.

O'Connor quickly developed a reputation for independence; she could not be easily categorized by political

In her early political life, O'Connor favored the Equal Rights Amendment (ERA). Marches in state capitals around the country, such as this one in Springfield, Illinois, were organized to encourage legislators to pass the amendment.

observers. By her own account, she was a *"fiscal* conservative and moderate Republican." Unlike many politicians, she was as careful about spending the state's money as she was about spending her own. Like many Westerners, and Republicans, she strongly supported the death penalty and vigorously opposed most gun-control laws.

In some ways, however, Sandra Day O'Connor's views seemed more liberal. During those years, for example, she was a strong supporter of the proposed Equal Rights Amendment (ERA), which would have prohibited the federal and state governments from discriminating on the basis of sex. She voted for strong environmental laws in Arizona and for many social welfare bills that protected groups typically powerless in the system, such as migrant farm workers and patients in mental institutions.

When it came to the issue of abortion, O'Connor was equally hard to classify. She supported laws to make information about birth control, including information about abortion, available to patients in public clinics, but opposed state funding for abortions and stated openly her personal opposition to abortion.

In 1970, the term of her appointment nearing an end, Sandra Day O'Connor ran for election for the first time in her life. She won the election, and another in 1972. Then, after just three years in the legislature, O'Connor was chosen by her colleagues to be the Arizona State Senate *majority leader* and became the first woman ever to serve in that position. As majority leader, she was exceptionally detail-conscious, thorough, and effective. However, the exhausting pace of elective politics was taking its toll on Sandra Day O'Connor and her family. She decided not to seek reelection but to return to law.

In 1974, she ran for a judge's seat on the Maricopa County Superior Court. Maricopa County, with more than two million residents, is Arizona's largest county. More than half of the entire Arizona population lives there, and its superior court is equal in stature to the highest courts of many small states. In some states, judgeships are filled by *legislative* or *executive appointment*. But in Arizona, the *trial court judges* are elected, and O'Connor, already a skilled campaigner, was well prepared for the race.

Although Phoenix had once been a quiet, peaceful city, in 1974 it had become so crime-ridden, many residents were afraid to leave their homes after dark. Running on a "law and order" platform, O'Connor promised stiff sentences to those convicted in her courtroom. She struck a chord with the voters and won the election, unseating an *incumbent* judge.

As legislator or judge, Sandra Day O'Connor had the same reputation: well informed, precise, efficient, and businesslike. Judge O'Connor made sure that the protections of the law were not denied to any defendant who came before her. She made it perfectly clear that it was more acceptable to have an admitted murderer freed than the rights of a defendant violated to obtain a conviction. On the other hand, Judge O'Connor did not hesitate to impose

After six years in the Arizona State Senate, Sandra Day O'Connor traded in her legislative duties for judge's robes. She took her seat on the Maricopa County Superior Court in 1974. The courthouse, in Phoenix, is pictured here.

Arizona Court of Appeals judge
O'Connor takes a break from work.

the death penalty under certain circumstances. She respected the law, and was not afraid to carry out its effects fully.

In one case, a woman was brought before Judge O'Connor for writing checks without money in her bank account to cover them. Abandoned by her husband and left with two small children, the woman, in desperation, had written checks totaling $3,500 after the failure of her business. In many states, writing bad checks is not considered a serious crime and is seldom brought to trial; few judges would sentence the defendant to a single day in jail. Judge O'Connor, however, sentenced the woman to five to ten years in prison, a longer sentence than many murderers receive. Although Sandra Day O'Connor acted within the legal framework for sentencing, many felt she was overly harsh under the circumstances. The ruling may have indicated O'Connor's deep-rooted belief that people must be held accountable for their actions.

In 1978, a Democrat named Bruce Babbitt was running for governor of Arizona and the Republican party urged Judge Sandra Day O'Connor to seek the Republican nomination. Although she still had political ambitions, she recognized Babbitt's popularity with the voters and declined to run. It was a wise decision, because less than a year later, Governor Babbitt appointed Sandra Day O'Connor to the Arizona Court of Appeals, the state's highest judicial body.

President Ronald Reagan strolls through the Rose Garden of the White House with his nominee Judge O'Connor.

CHAPTER 5

LIFE ON THE
U.S. SUPREME COURT

After only a few months in office, Republican President Ronald Reagan had the opportunity to fulfill a campaign promise: to nominate the first woman ever to serve on the Supreme Court. Over one hundred justices had served on the Court since its establishment in 1789, but all of them had been men. When Associate Justice Potter Stewart, who had been appointed to the Court in 1958 by President Eisenhower, notified Reagan of his intention to retire in 1981, the president ordered his top aides to begin the search for a suitable replacement. Of the several dozen names discussed, only one of the potential nominees was invited to the White House to meet with the president. He met privately with that candidate for less than an hour. On July 7, 1981, President Reagan announced the nomination of Judge Sandra Day O'Connor to the U.S. Supreme Court.

When appointed as *appellate judge* on the Arizona Court of Appeals, Sandra Day O'Connor might have thought she had reached the peak of her judicial career. A well-respected judge in her home state, she was perfectly content to live close to family and friends on the same land that she had loved as a child and to which she had returned as an adult. When President Reagan called on her to serve on the Court, she must have been overwhelmed with pride, excitement, and anxiety. Her nomination to the Supreme Court changed not only her and her family's lives, but also American history and the role of women in it.

Before taking a seat on the bench, however, Judge Sandra Day O'Connor had to appear before the U.S. Senate Judiciary Committee and receive approval from the entire Senate. The committee members had many questions for the nominee, especially about her views on abortion. *Roe v. Wade*, a 1973 case securing a woman's right to have an abortion under certain circumstances, was in danger of being overturned. Despite the insistent questioning of several senators, Sandra Day O'Connor refused to say how she would rule on particular matters that could come before the Court, including a challenge to *Roe v. Wade*. She did, however, express her personal opposition to abortion, and her belief that the Congress, not the courts, should handle the issue.

After a few days of questioning, the Senate Judiciary Committee approved her nomination. The next step was a vote before the full Senate. Ninety-nine senators voted

Justice O'Connor with (clockwise) her husband, John, and sons, Jay, Brian, and Scott, in the summer of 1981.

to confirm her nomination and one did not vote. Sandra Day O'Connor was sworn in as the nation's first woman Supreme Court justice on September 25, 1981.

President Reagan appreciated O'Connor's conservative, Republican background and chose her with the hope that she would support her party's positions from the bench. Like many Republicans, O'Connor believed strongly in what is called *judicial restraint*, the concept that the courts should not act as a legislative body. However, as a judge, O'Connor had ruled in accordance with her own conscience and stuck to no party line. There was no sign that as a justice she would do otherwise. In fact, her rulings on any single issue were often difficult to predict.

In two 1988 cases related to freedom of speech, Justice O'Connor showed her willingness to see both sides of an issue. The first, *Boos v. Barry*, challenged a Washington, D.C., law that prohibited political demonstrations near the embassies of foreign governments. The *First Amendment* of the U.S. Constitution provides for free speech, and the Court closely examines any law that attempts to regulate speech. The majority of justices struck down the law in an opinion written by Justice O'Connor, who stated that political protest was "at the core of the First Amendment." Interestingly, O'Connor was at odds with her old friend and classmate Chief Justice William H. Rehnquist, who voted to uphold the law.

In the second case, which again tested the limits of

After Senate approval of her historic nomination, Sandra Day O'Connor waves on the steps of the U.S. Capitol. Next to her on the left is Senator Barry Goldwater of Arizona, and on the right then Vice President George Bush.

free speech, O'Connor offered a different opinion. *Hazelwood School District v. Kuhlmeier* involved an action brought by the student editor of a public high school newspaper who had written articles about pregnant students and students with divorced parents. The principal considered the material objectionable and deleted the stories. The student sued the school district, claiming that her First Amendment rights had been violated. O'Connor joined with Rehnquist and others in a majority opinion that upheld the principal's actions, saying that schools have the right to oversee "school-sponsored expressive activities."

On the issue of *affirmative action*, like free speech, Justice O'Connor made her decisions case-by-case. In one well-publicized case in 1987, *Johnson v. Transportation of Santa Clara County*, a California man named Paul Johnson challenged an affirmative action plan that gave preference to another worker simply because of her gender. Despite Paul Johnson's experience and slightly higher scores on the agency examination, the female applicant was given the supervisory position.

Although the Reagan administration supported Johnson's argument, the Court rejected it. Justice O'Connor joined with the majority. She also stated in a separate opinion that employers should be free to adopt affirmative action plans if they had a "firm basis" for believing past discrimination had occurred. Convinced that any

In addition to her work on the Court, Sandra Day O'Connor frequently makes appearances and delivers speeches. Here, she accepts an honorary law degree from the University of Minnesota in 1987.

discrimination violates federal law, Justice Antonin Scalia, another member of the Court, was furious at the decision. He was particularly displeased with O'Connor for not committing to one position and for trying to find compromises on important issues. To Justice Scalia, finding a "middle ground" was the job of a politician, not a judge.

In a 1989 case, *Richmond v. J.A. Croson Company*, Justice O'Connor voted against affirmative action. She wrote the Court's majority opinion, which struck down a Virginia law requiring that 30 percent of the city's contracting work be reserved for firms owned by African Americans, Hispanics, or other minority-group members. With no basis for the percentage itself and no evidence linking past discrimination to the plan, the law appeared random and unreasonable. The Court's opinion made it clear that governmental discrimination against whites violated the Constitution just as much as discrimination against blacks.

Justice O'Connor's opinion allowed for racial preferences when past discrimination could be proven and the remedy appeared to be reasonable. Again, she met with strong disagreement from Justice Scalia and the Court's other true conservatives, who wanted to end racial preferences in every instance.

Justice O'Connor's votes in cases that dealt with criminal law and the death penalty were her most predictable

A former law professor, Justice Antonin Scalia is known for his strongly held opinions, sometimes in direct opposition to those of the other justices on the bench.

decisions. She had a generally unforgiving view of criminals, whatever their circumstances. She also believed in limiting Constitutional protections available to defendants in state courts.

Harmelin v. Michigan was a 1991 case brought by a Michigan prisoner who challenged the severity of his sentence. A U.S. Air Force veteran, Ronald Harmelin, had been sentenced to life in prison without the possibility of parole after he was convicted of cocaine possession. If he had committed murder in the state of Michigan, he could not have received a harsher sentence. Justice O'Connor voted with the majority, which declared Harmelin's claim, that his sentence violated the *Eighth Amendment* of the U.S. Constitution because it was cruel and unusual, had no merit.

In other cases involving the overturning of convicts' death sentences, O'Connor continued to side with the conservative block, but she occasionally voted with the liberals in other criminals' rights cases. In one 1988 case, *Thompson v. Oklahoma,* the state of Oklahoma wanted to execute William Wayne Thompson for committing murder at the age of fifteen. Thompson claimed his motivation for the act was the victim's continued abuse of his wife, who was Thompson's sister. O'Connor's vote against the young man's execution saved his life.

Since Sandra Day O'Connor's appointment to the Supreme Court, several major challenges to *Roe v. Wade*

have been brought before it. Though personally opposed to abortion, O'Connor resisted joining in opinions that would have reversed *Roe v. Wade*. However, she has consistently voted to uphold state laws that restrict the protections originally granted by *Roe*.

Sandra Day O'Connor's legacy to the Supreme Court and to the people of the United States is unique. As the first woman to serve on the Supreme Court, she helped to tear down a barrier that had stood for nearly two centuries. Plenty of American women had served as governors, ambassadors, legislators, and judges. The country's highest court, however, had remained an all-male establishment for more than sixty years after the Constitution was amended to allow women to vote.

O'Connor's presence on the Supreme Court proved that women judges are worthy of the same respect and admiration as their male peers. Like any judge, she based her opinions on her perception of the facts and her application of the relevant laws. And on the bench, Sandra Day O'Connor formed her opinions as a woman justice, not as "the women's justice."

Sandra Day O'Connor deserves respect for another, more unfortunate, reason. Like millions of other women, O'Connor was confronted with the harsh reality of breast cancer, which was diagnosed in 1988. For a short time, she might have been tempted to resign from the Court and return home to Arizona and her circle of family and

Sandra Day O'Connor has impressively handled the consid-erable public attention, pressures, and responsibilities of being the first woman to serve on the Supreme Court.

friends. Giving up, however, had never been part of O'Connor's nature. Despite undergoing surgery and other forms of treatment, she has remained on the Supreme Court and continued to work seventy-hour weeks. Today, Justice Sandra Day O'Connor is still hard at work, helping to make the decisions that will shape American life long after the end of her judicial career.

The Supreme Court, 1981
(clockwise from upper left) Associate Justices John Paul
Stevens, Lewis F. Powell, Jr., William H. Rehnquist, Sandra
Day O'Connor, Harry A. Blackmun, and Byron R. White,
Chief Justice Warren E. Burger, and Associate Justices
William J. Brennan, Jr. and Thurgood Marshall

GLOSSARY

Affirmative action — a preferential granting of educational benefits or employment opportunities to members of a minority group, or women.

Appellate judge — a judge who sits on a court of appeals, which is superior to a general trial court, and mostly reviews the decisions of lower courts to determine whether the trial was fair and the ruling constitutional.

Appointment (executive or legislative) — in state politics, the naming of an individual to a government position by either the governor or the state legislature.

Bar — a group of lawyers admitted to the practice of law.

Criminal defense attorney — a lawyer who works to protect the rights of an individual accused of committing crimes and represents that person in court.

Eighth Amendment — a part of the Bill of Rights (the original ten amendments to the Constitution), which bans unreasonable bail for defendants, excessive fines, and "cruel and unusual punishments" for crimes committed.

First Amendment — a part of the Bill of Rights (the original ten amendments to the Constitution), which protects freedom of religion, speech, and press and the right to demonstrate against the government's policies.

Fiscal — relating to money.

Incumbent — an official who presently holds government office.

Judicial restraint — the theory that a court should not let personal opinion affect its decisions and that a judge should not interfere with legislative policies unless the policies violate the Constitution.

Majority leader — the head of the political party with the most seats in a legislative body.

Prosecutor — a government lawyer who tries cases against people accused of violating criminal laws.

State attorney general — a usually elected public official who represents the state in criminal or civil matters.

State legislature — the lawmaking branch of state government usually made up of two houses, the state senate and the state house of representatives.

Trial court judge — a judge who presides over a general trial court, which may hear criminal or civil cases.

FOR FURTHER READING

Aria, Barbara. *The Supreme Court*. New York: Franklin Watts, 1994.

Gherman, Beverly. *Sandra Day O'Connor: Justice for All*. New York: Viking, 1991.

Henry, Christopher. *Ruth Bader Ginsburg*. New York: Franklin Watts, 1994.

Huber, Peter W. *Sandra Day O'Connor*. New York: Chelsea House, 1990.

Macht, Norman L. *Sandra Day O'Connor*. New York: Chelsea House, 1992.

Reef, Catherine. *The Supreme Court*. New York: Dillon, 1994.

INDEX

ABOUT THE AUTHOR

Christopher Henry is a New York attorney in private practice. He is the author of two books about American immigration law and several books for children, including biographies of Ben Nighthorse Campbell and Henry Cisneros. He has also written the Watts First Book biography *Ruth Bader Ginsburg*.